*From* The MAILBOX®

# APRIL

## A MONTH OF REPRODUCIBLES AT YOUR FINGERTIPS!

Grades
2–3

D1410552

### Project Editor
Darcy Brown

### Writers
Darcy Brown, Stacie Stone Davis, Allison White Haynes,
Cynthia Holcomb, Susan Hohbach Walker

### Art Coordinator
Clevell Harris

### Artists
Cathy Spangler Bruce, Clevell Harris, Mary Lester,
Rob Mayworth, Kimberly Richard, Rebecca Saunders,
Barry Slate, Donna K. Teal

### Cover Artist
Jennifer Tipton Bennett

www.themailbox.com

©1998 by THE EDUCATION CENTER, INC.
All rights reserved.
ISBN #1-56234-232-0

Manufactured in the United States

10 9 8 7 6 5 4 3

# Table Of Contents

# April Free Time

| Monday | Tuesday | Wednesday | Thursday | Friday |
|---|---|---|---|---|
| Celebrate April Fools' Day on April 1. Write a story about a time you were silly.  | The first movie theater opened on April 2, 1902. Write a paragraph about your favorite movie.  | April is National Automobile Month. Design a car that you would like to drive in the future. | April 4 is National Reading A Road Map Day. Draw a map of your neighborhood; then give it to a friend to read. Our Neighborhood Map  | The first modern Olympic® Games began in Athens, Greece, on April 6, 1896. List your favorite Olympic® events. |
| World Health Day (April 7) was started by the World Health Organization. Make a poster to promote good health habits. 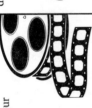 | National Lawn and Garden Month is held during April. List five foods you enjoy eating that come from a garden. | Beverly Clearly, the famous author of children's books, was born on April 12, 1916. List your favorite books by this author. | Celebrate Astronomy Week (dates vary). Can you name one of the many constellations in our galaxy? Draw an outline of your favorite one.  | Thomas Jefferson, America's third president, was born on April 13, 1743. List the names of other presidents you know.  |
| Thank You School Librarian Day, celebrated on the Wednesday of National Library Week, is the perfect chance for you to tell your librarian how special he or she is. Design a bookmark in his or her honor. | The third Tuesday in April is Look-Alike Day. Your best look-alike is your reflection. Imagine you are looking into a mirror; then draw a picture of yourself. | Paul Revere began his famous ride late at night on April 18, 1775. Write about the warning he brought to the American patriots. | April is Math Education Month. Create a math word problem about something that happened to you in school this week.  | April 22 is Earth Day. Write about a way you can help the earth today. |
| The first public school in the United States opened on April 23, 1635. Write a make-believe story about the day your school opened.  | Buddy, the first guide dog, was paired with its blind owner on April 25, 1928. List other things that are helpful to a blind person. | On April 29, 1913, the first zipper was patented. List some other inventions that we use every day. | Tell the truth! April 30 is National Honesty Day. Write a story about a time when you were honest. **HONESTY!** | National Arbor Day is celebrated by most states on the last Friday in April. This day is for honoring trees. List ten ways a tree may be used. |

**Note To The Teacher:** Have each student staple a copy of this page inside a file folder. Direct students to store their completed work in their folders.

# April
## Events And Activities For The Family

**Directions:** Select at least one activity below to complete as a family by the end of April.

### National Humor Month

Celebrate National Humor Month by sending your family members on a hunt for humor. Have each family member scan children's magazines, age-appropriate television programs, and favorite books for bits of humor. Talk about the humor found in each item. After the discussion, create a humor collage by gluing humorous pictures to a large piece of poster board. For added enjoyment, have each family member express her own sense of humor. Challenge her to write or tell a joke or a funny story, put on a silly show, or draw a humorous picture. You can count on plenty of knee-slapping fun!

### ZAM! Zoo And Aquarium Month

This monthlong celebration, sponsored by the American Zoo and Aquarium Association, is held as an effort to emphasize the important roles zoos and aquariums play in wildlife education. Provide a firsthand look at animals and their habitats with a family trip to a local zoo or aquarium. Arrange for a zookeeper or another staff member to talk with your family during or prior to your visit. After the trip, have each family member research a different animal, then write a factual report or find literature or pictures pertaining to the animal. Then set up the items in your family room for a simply wild display!

### Keep America Beautiful Month

Encourage your family to lend a hand during Keep America Beautiful Month. Check with a local service agency to find out about ongoing cleanup projects in your area. Have your family members spend an hour helping to pick up trash at a designated site. (Check the area for possible dangers prior to taking your family.) With many helping hands, much can be accomplished in a short time. Your family will be glad to know they helped in keeping America beautiful.

# Plip, Plop, Raindrops!

April showers bring May flowers…
and *lots* of learning experiences.
Shower your youngsters with this pitter-patter
of exciting activities.

## Wonderful Rain!

Add a splash to any rainy day by sharing this collection of facts.

- Raindrops form when frozen precipitation melts or when water droplets in clouds combine.
- Raindrops vary in size from .02 to .25 inches in diameter.
- The size of a raindrop determines its speed—the larger the drop, the faster it falls to the earth.
- Animals, humans, and plants need water to survive.
- Rain helps clean the air by washing away dust and chemical pollutants.
- Too much rain may cause flooding, damage crops, and destroy property.
- Rain can be measured with a *rain gauge* or by using *radar.*

After sharing the facts, have each pair of students copy a different fact onto a light blue construction-paper raindrop. (Some students may copy the same fact.) Next have each pair illustrate its fact on drawing paper. Invite each pair to share its drawing with its classmates. Collect the raindrops and the drawings; then mount them around an umbrella cutout on a bulletin board titled "Wonderful Rain!" Conclude the activity by having each student name one way rain is important in nature.

## Pitter-Patter, Plip-Plop

Who can resist the soothing sounds of rain? Re-create these sounds in your classroom by having each youngster make a rain stick. To make a rain stick, a student pushes ten brads randomly into a paper-towel tube. (He may need assistance with this step.) Next he covers one end of the tube with a 3-inch square of construction paper and secures it with tape. He then fills his tube with 1/4 cup of rice and secures the other end of the tube in the same manner. He decorates an 11" x 6" piece of construction paper; then he glues the paper to his tube. When the glue has dried, invite each youngster to turn his rainstick over so he may enjoy the sound of falling rain. If desired, have students use the rainsticks as they perform their dances in "Let's Dance!"

## Let's Dance!

The rain dance, performed by the American Indians of the Southwestern United States, is a ceremony held during the spring planting season and during the summer. Each Indian tribe has its own ceremony asking spirits to send rain for its crops. After telling youngsters about these interesting ceremonies, have small groups of students create their own rain dances. Set a time limit; then let the creating begin. When time has expired, play some lively instrumental music and invite each group, in turn, to perform its rain dance for the class. Let the rain dance begin!

_____

_____

_____

_____

_____

_____

_____

_____

_____

_____

_____

_____

_____

_____

**Note To The Teacher:** Duplicate one copy of this page for each student. Have each youngster write a rainy-day story on the lines and color the page as desired. Bind the stories between two construction-paper covers titled "Rainy-Day Adventures" or mount them on a bulletin board titled "Down Came The Rain."

# Undercover Contractions

Use the words on each umbrella to make a contraction.
Write each contraction on the correct line below.

1. there is
2. he will
3. will not
4. you have
5. she is
6. I am
7. that is
8. have not
9. who is
10. we have
11. they would
12. can not

1. _____    5. _____    9. _____

2. _____    6. _____    10. _____

3. _____    7. _____    11. _____

4. _____    8. _____    12. _____

**Bonus Box:** On the back of this sheet, write a rainy-day story that includes five contractions from above.

Name _____

# Rain, Rain, Go Away!

Answer the questions.
Use the bar graph.

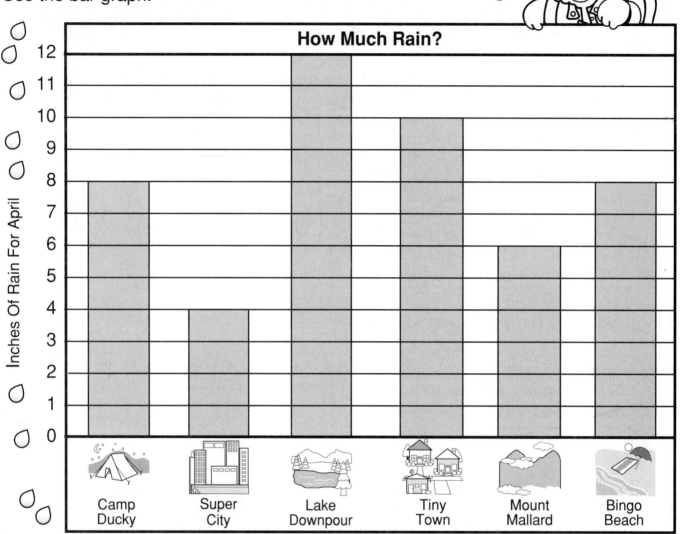

1. Which place received the most amount of rain? _____

2. Which place received the least amount of rain: Mount Mallard or Camp Ducky? _____

3. How many inches of rain did Super City and Bingo Beach receive altogether? _____

4. How many inches of rain did Lake Downpour and Tiny Town receive altogether? _____

5. How many more inches of rain did Camp Ducky receive than Super City? _____

6. How many more inches of rain did Lake Downpour receive than Bingo Beach? _____

7. How many inches of rain fell in all the places combined? (Use the back of this paper to add

the amounts together.) _____

**Bonus Box:** Choose a place from the graph. On another sheet of paper, write a story about the day it rained 20 inches.

©1998 The Education Center, Inc. • *April Monthly Reproducibles* • Grades 2–3 • TEC949 • Key p. 63

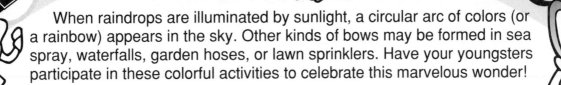

# Rainbow Days

When raindrops are illuminated by sunlight, a circular arc of colors (or a rainbow) appears in the sky. Other kinds of bows may be formed in sea spray, waterfalls, garden hoses, or lawn sprinklers. Have your youngsters participate in these colorful activities to celebrate this marvelous wonder!

## The End Of The Rainbow

What can you find at the end of a rainbow? A pot of gold, of course! After discussing this legend, have youngsters create these beautiful projects. First duplicate one copy of the cloud and pot patterns (page 10) for each child. To make the project, each student completes the sentence on her pot, writes her name on the line, and then colors and cuts out the cloud and the pot. Next she draws a rainbow outline (like the one shown) on a 9" x 12" sheet of white construction paper and paints it as desired. She glues cotton balls to her cloud pattern and sets it aside. Next she applies glue to the shaded part of her pot; then she sprinkles gold glitter atop the glue. To assemble the project, she cuts out her rainbow, then glues the cloud and pot patterns to each end of the rainbow as shown. Display the projects around the room for all to enjoy.

When I got to the end of the rainbow…

Benjamin S.

## Blossoming Rainbows

Brighten your classroom with these beautiful blossoms! Each student will need six coffee filters, one 5-inch green pipe cleaner, masking tape, and access to rainbow-colored markers—*red, orange, yellow, green, blue,* and *purple.* To make his blossom, a youngster outlines the edge of each filter with a different color marker. He stacks the filters atop each other in rainbow-color order; then he pinches the centers together. Next he bends the pipe cleaner in half and slips the pinched end of the blossom between the ends of the pipe cleaner. He then wraps tape around the pipe cleaner ends to hold the flower in place. To complete the project, he carefully pulls apart the coffee filters to open the flower. Beautiful!

## Colorful Division

Review division facts with a game of Colorful Division. To begin, pair students; then give each pair a copy of the game on page 11. Have students cut out the pocket and the cards and assemble them as directed. To play the game, each student, in turn, selects a card from the pocket, reads the fact printed on it, and solves the problem. If the child is correct, he colors the coin that has the corresponding answer. If he's incorrect, he asks his partner for help; then he colors the matching coin. (For ease in checking answers, you may wish to provide each pair with a copy of the answer key on page 63.) To meet individual needs, duplicate one copy of the reproducible. White-out all the math facts and answers, then duplicate a class supply. Next distribute one copy to each child. Instruct him to program the math fact cards with division facts he needs to practice; then direct him to program the coins with the corresponding answers.

9

# Cloud And Pot Patterns

When I got to the end of the rainbow…

Name

©1998 The Education Center, Inc. • *April Monthly Reproducibles* • Grades 2–3 • TEC949

3 1833 05027 6259

**Note To The Teacher:** See "The End Of The Rainbow" on page 9 for directions on how to use these patterns.

# Colorful Division

## Directions:

1. Cut out the pocket. Glue the pocket onto the paper.
2. Cut out the fact cards. Put them in the pocket.
3. Take turns picking a fact card. Tell your partner the answer.
4. Then color a matching coin.

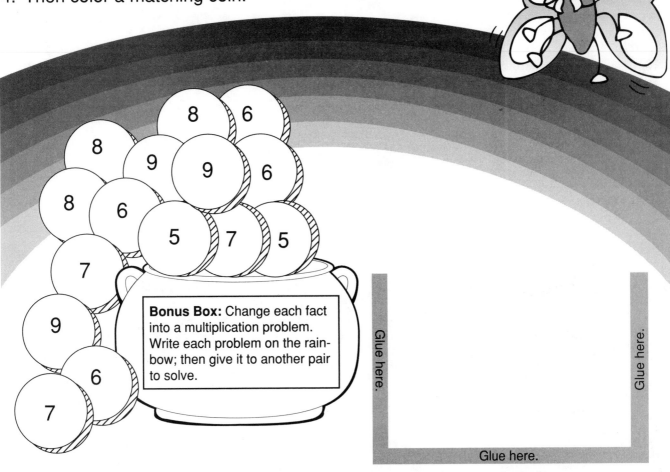

**Bonus Box:** Change each fact into a multiplication problem. Write each problem on the rainbow; then give it to another pair to solve.

Glue here.

Glue here.

Glue here.

©1998 The Education Center, Inc. • *April Monthly Reproducibles* • Grades 2–3 • TEC949

### Division Facts

| 25 ÷ 5 | 72 ÷ 8 | 48 ÷ 6 | 63 ÷ 9 |
| 64 ÷ 8 | 40 ÷ 8 | 63 ÷ 7 | 40 ÷ 5 |

| 36 ÷ 6 | 54 ÷ 9 | 81 ÷ 9 | 56 ÷ 8 | 35 ÷ 7 | 42 ÷ 7 | 49 ÷ 7 |

**Note To The Teacher:** Use with "Colorful Division" on page 9.

11

Name_____

# Somewhere Over The Rainbow

Circle the factors on the clouds to complete each multiplication problem.
The first one has been done for you.

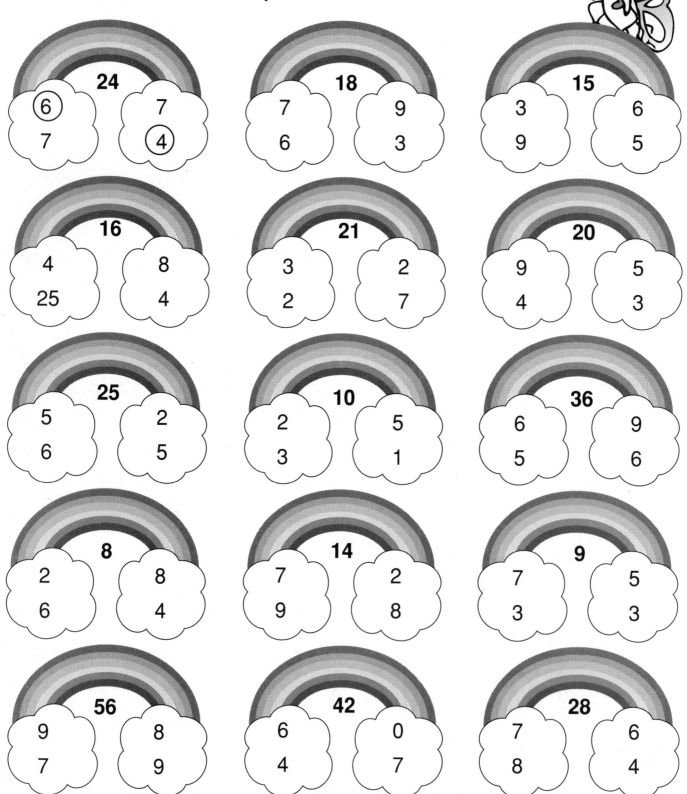

**24**
(6) 7
7 (4)

**18**
7 9
6 3

**15**
3 6
9 5

**16**
4 8
25 4

**21**
3 2
2 7

**20**
9 5
4 3

**25**
5 2
6 5

**10**
2 5
3 1

**36**
6 9
5 6

**8**
2 8
6 4

**14**
7 2
9 8

**9**
7 5
3 3

**56**
9 8
7 9

**42**
6 0
4 7

**28**
7 6
8 4

**Bonus Box:** On the back of this paper, write 15 multiplication problems for the factors *not circled* on each cloud.

# HOORAY FOR EARTH DAY!

Earth Day, first celebrated on April 22, 1970, is observed to remind us of the importance of preserving the natural resources in our environment. This day calls attention to the needs of protecting clean water, healthy trees, and fresh air. No doubt your little environmentalists will give a hip, hip, hooray for Earth Day!

## Save The Earth!

Enhance your youngsters' environmental awareness by sharing Laura Lee Benson's book *This Is Our Earth* (Charlesbridge Publishing, Inc.; 1994). Next provide each youngster with one construction-paper copy each of the earth and writing patterns on pages 14 and 15. Instruct each child to write about one way she can save the earth on each of her writing patterns. Next direct her to write her name on her earth pattern, and to color the earth and arm patterns as desired. Then have her cut out all the patterns. Have her apply glue to the shaded part of the arm patterns and then attach them to the sides of her earth. To complete the project, instruct her to tape a 16-inch length of yarn to the bottom of her earth, then evenly tape each writing pattern to the yarn. Invite students to share their projects with their classmates; then display them around the room as reminders to save the earth!

## A Pledge To Save

As a culminating activity, have youngsters make a pledge to save the earth. Give each student a copy of the "Save The Earth Pledge" on page 16. Sing the pledge (adapted to the tune of "Row, Row, Row Your Boat") or read it aloud as your class follows along. Talk with students about what the pledge means; then ask each child to sign his name and write the date on the lines. If desired have youngsters mount their pledges on slightly larger sheets of construction paper. Challenge students to memorize the pledge, then sing or recite it to classmates. You can count on your little earth-friendly citizens to do their part and save the earth!

## Junk Art

Encourage students to reuse recyclable items by creating junk art. To begin, ask students to bring to school recyclable items, such as paper-towel rolls, plastic six-pack rings, newspapers, plastic milk jugs and soda bottles, foam packaging, aluminum foil, fabric scraps, cardboard and foam egg cartons, and cardboard boxes. Challenge youngsters to use the items to create a unique project. Invite each child to share his creation with his classmates. If desired award youngsters for *Most Creative Project, Most Unusual Project, Most Recycled Items Used,* and *Most Useful Project.*

13

## Save
## The Earth!

_____
name

**Note To The Teacher:** Use with "Save The Earth!" on page 13.

**Note To The Teacher:** Use with "Save The Earth!" on page 13.

# Save The Earth!

Save, save, save the earth.
Recycle every day.
To pick up trash and do my part,
Is what I pledge today.

_____
Name

_____
Date

©1998 The Education Center, Inc. • *April Monthly Reproducibles* • Grades 2–3 • TEC949

# Save The Earth!

Save, save, save the earth.
Recycle every day.
To pick up trash and do my part,
Is what I pledge today.

_____
Name

_____
Date

©1998 The Education Center, Inc. • *April Monthly Reproducibles* • Grades 2–3 • TEC949

Name _____

# Protect Our Planet

Color the earths. Use the code.
Explain each answer on the lines.

 Pick up trash and throw it away. _____

_____

 Use only one side of a piece of paper. _____

_____

 Walk or ride a bike instead of riding in the car. _____

_____

 It's important to recycle. _____

_____

 Leave the water running while brushing your teeth. _____

_____

 Respect the habitats of wildlife. _____

_____

 A little bit of littering is OK. _____

_____

Save The Earth!

**Bonus Box:** On the back of this paper, draw and color a picture that illustrates one sentence from above.

17

Name _____

# Ready, Set, Recycle!

Cut out the boxes below.
Sort the boxes by recycling material.
Glue each box onto the correct bin.

Paper And
Cardboard

Aluminum
And Tin

Glass And
Plastic

**Bonus Box:** Look at the pictures on the leftover boxes. These can be used to make *compost*—an organic fertilizer. On the back of this page, draw your own compost pile. Glue the pictures to the top of the pile.

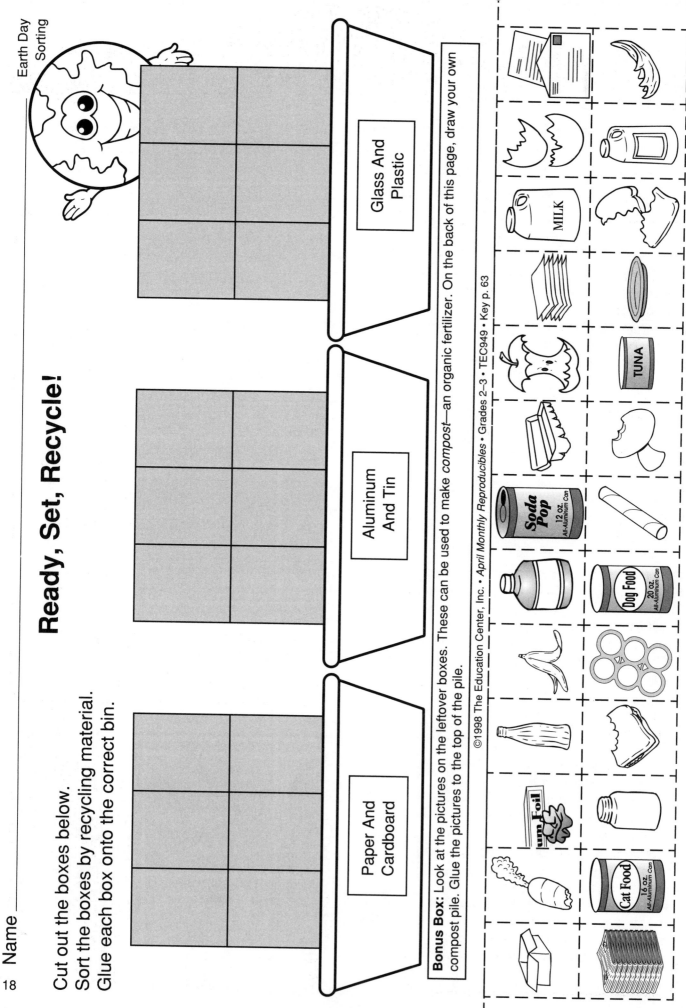

# "TREE-MENDOUS" TREES

With the first green leaves of spring unfolding and the observance of National Arbor Day, April lends itself to a closer look at trees. Most states observe Arbor Day on the last Friday in April, but with the following activities and reproducibles, you can celebrate from trunk to treetop all month long.

## State Your Tree

What's one thing that makes your state great? Your state tree, of course! Have your students research to find which tree is honored in your state. Help them discover when the tree was selected by the state, why it was chosen, and other interesting facts. If possible, take your class to see a nearby example of the tree. Then have each student make a poster telling about the tree. Display the completed posters for a forest of facts about your state foliage!

State: Texas
Tree: Pecan
Fact: Pecans are used to make pecan pie.

## Love Those Leaves!

As the days of April pass, your students will notice that the trees are beginning to put out more and more leaves. Explain to students that leaves are the "food factories" for most trees. And in addition to making food for the trees, leaves help control the exchange of gases as trees take in carbon dioxide and release oxygen. Leaves also help maintain the water system for the tree; they have small openings called *stomata* that control the amount of water loss during drier times.

Encourage your students to start a class leaf collection by asking them to bring to school a variety of leaves or pictures of leaves. Store the leaves and a magnifying glass in a center for students to observe. Have youngsters sort the leaves by color, texture, and size; then invite them to write their findings on provided paper. If possible, also include a resource book to help students identify the trees from which the leaves came.

## Terrific Trees

Why all this talk about trees? Your students need to be aware that trees are valuable to mankind because of their many products and because of ecological reasons. Share with your students these terrific tree tidbits; then reinforce the importance of these prominent plants by having each student make a booklet about trees. Distribute one copy of the booklet pages on pages 21 and 22 to each child. Ask each child to write his name on the booklet cover. As a class, read the fact on each page; then have each student complete the activity. Next distribute a construction-paper copy of the booklet pattern on page 20 to each youngster. Direct him to color and cut out his pattern; then have him cut out his booklet cover and booklet pages. Finally, have him stack the booklet cover and the booklet pages in sequential order; then staple the cover and the pages to the front of the pattern where indicated.

- Many trees are major sources of food, primarily fruits and nuts.
- Sugar is derived from the sap of some trees.
- Wood is still a major source of fuel for heating and cooking.
- Lumber, plywood, and particle board are valuable construction materials.
- Paper comes from wood fiber.
- Fibers, such as rayon, are produced from wood pulp.
- Root systems help protect soil from erosion.
- Trees create wildlife habitats.
- Trees provide shade and beauty to landscaping.

# Tree Booklet Patterns

Staple here.

Hug a tree today!

©1998 The Education Center, Inc.

Staple here.

Hug a tree today!

©1998 The Education Center, Inc.

**Note To The Teacher:** Use with "Terrific Trees" on page 19.

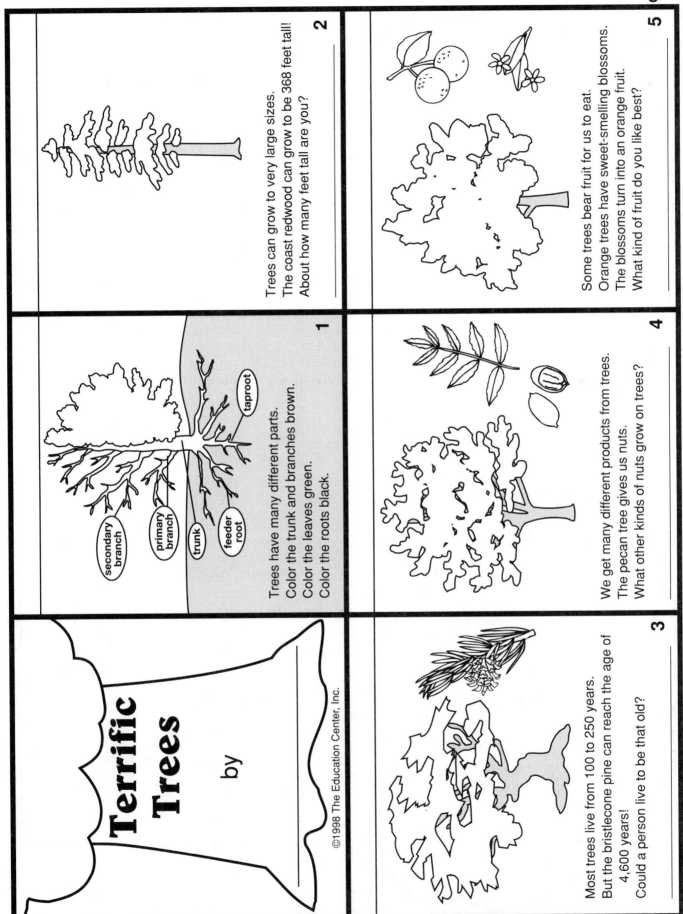

**2**

Trees can grow to very large sizes.
The coast redwood can grow to be 368 feet tall!
About how many feet tall are you?

**5**

Some trees bear fruit for us to eat.
Orange trees have sweet-smelling blossoms.
The blossoms turn into an orange fruit.
What kind of fruit do you like best?

**1**

secondary branch
primary branch
trunk
feeder root
taproot

Trees have many different parts.
Color the trunk and branches brown.
Color the leaves green.
Color the roots black.

**4**

We get many different products from trees.
The pecan tree gives us nuts.
What other kinds of nuts grow on trees?

# Terrific Trees

by

**3**

Most trees live from 100 to 250 years.
But the bristlecone pine can reach the age of 4,600 years!
Could a person live to be that old?

**Note To The Teacher:** Use with "Terrific Trees" on page 19.

# Booklet Pages

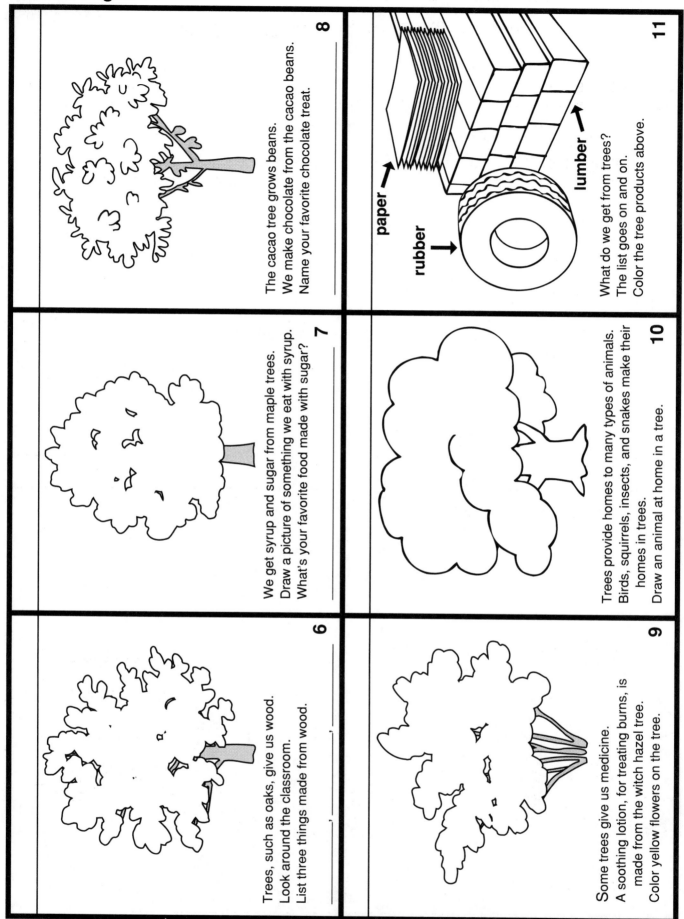

**8**

The cacao tree grows beans.
We make chocolate from the cacao beans.
Name your favorite chocolate treat.

**11**

paper →

rubber →

← lumber

What do we get from trees?
The list goes on and on.
Color the tree products above.

**7**

We get syrup and sugar from maple trees.
Draw a picture of something we eat with syrup.
What's your favorite food made with sugar?

**10**

Trees provide homes to many types of animals.
Birds, squirrels, insects, and snakes make their homes in trees.
Draw an animal at home in a tree.

**6**

Trees, such as oaks, give us wood.
Look around the classroom.
List three things made from wood.

**9**

Some trees give us medicine.
A soothing lotion, for treating burns, is made from the witch hazel tree.
Color yellow flowers on the tree.

# Leafing Through The Dictionary

Study the dictionary entry below.
Follow each step.
Lightly color the leaf when you finish each step.

> **tree** (trē) *noun* A woody plant having a single main stem. It can reach heights of 20 to 25 feet and live for many years.

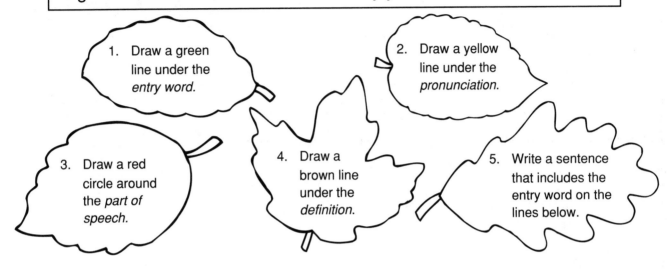

1. Draw a green line under the *entry word.*

2. Draw a yellow line under the *pronunciation.*

3. Draw a red circle around the *part of speech.*

4. Draw a brown line under the *definition.*

5. Write a sentence that includes the entry word on the lines below.

_____

_____

Read the guide words on each leaf.
On the line write an entry word that would be on the same dictionary page as the
    guide words.

**Entry Words**

root
branch
maple
banana
fruit

fig • grapefruit

_____

redwood • rubber

_____

apple • bark

_____

beech • coconut

_____

lime • nut

_____

**Bonus Box:** On the back of this page, write the entry words in ABC order.

Name _____

# "Tree-mendous" Work!

Directions:

1. _____
2. _____
3. _____
4. _____
5. _____
6. _____
7. _____
8. _____
9. _____
10. _____
11. _____
12. _____

**Note To The Teacher:** Duplicate one copy of this page. Write the directions at the top. Program the leaves with words to put in alphabetical order; words to match with synonyms, antonyms, or homophones; or numerals, number words, or months to sequence. Then duplicate a class supply.

# JELLY BEAN JUBILEE!

"Bean" looking for a colorful way for students to brush up on basic skills?
Then these activities are just what you're looking for!
There's no doubt about it—jelly beans are just plain fun!

## Fun With Fractions

Tempt youngsters' taste buds with this fun fraction activity. Provide each child with a small jelly-bean-filled cupcake liner or small paper cup and a copy of "Colorful Fractions" on page 27. (Be sure that each container has an assortment of colored jelly beans.) Instruct each child to count the number of jelly beans in his set and record it on his paper. Explain to students that this number will be the *denominator*—the bottom number of the fraction. Then tell each student to count the number of red jelly beans in his set. After determining what fractional part of the set is red, have the student record this information on his paper. Have students repeat this process for each of the remaining jelly bean colors. Encourage students to complete their papers by adding the fractions together. Invite youngsters to munch on their jelly beans when they finish their papers. Yum!

## Jelly Bean Lotto

Get your students jumping with a fun game of jelly bean lotto! In advance draw an unprogrammed grid (see the example); then duplicate a class supply. Also draw a large jelly bean on a piece of chart paper. To begin, challenge students to brainstorm words that describe jelly beans; then write 16 responses on the chart-paper jelly bean. Next distribute a grid and 16 jelly beans to each student. Instruct her to randomly program each square with a different jelly bean word from the list. Then read aloud each word at random. Have each student cover the called-out word with a jelly bean. When she covers four in a row, she calls out "Lotto!" Challenge the winning student to use each of the four words in a sentence. Then have youngsters clear their boards for additional rounds.

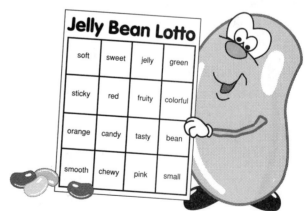

**Jelly Bean Lotto**

| soft | sweet | jelly | green |
| --- | --- | --- | --- |
| sticky | red | fruity | colorful |
| orange | candy | tasty | bean |
| smooth | chewy | pink | small |

## Jovial Jelly Beans

These jovial jelly beans are sure to brighten any classroom! Provide each child with a white construction-paper copy of the jelly bean pattern on page 26. Instruct each youngster to write a jelly bean story on the lines, then illustrate the pattern as desired. (If desired, have him incorporate some of the jelly bean words from "Jelly Bean Lotto" into his story.) Next direct each student to cover his jelly bean with colored plastic wrap; then secure the wrap to the back of the jelly bean with tape. Invite youngsters to share their stories with their classmates. Then collect the projects and display them around the room for all to enjoy!

One day I came home from school to find a giant pile of jelly beans in my yard! They were all colors. I was so excited, that I began to eat them. Boy, did my tummy hurt!
Jason

25

# Jelly Bean Pattern

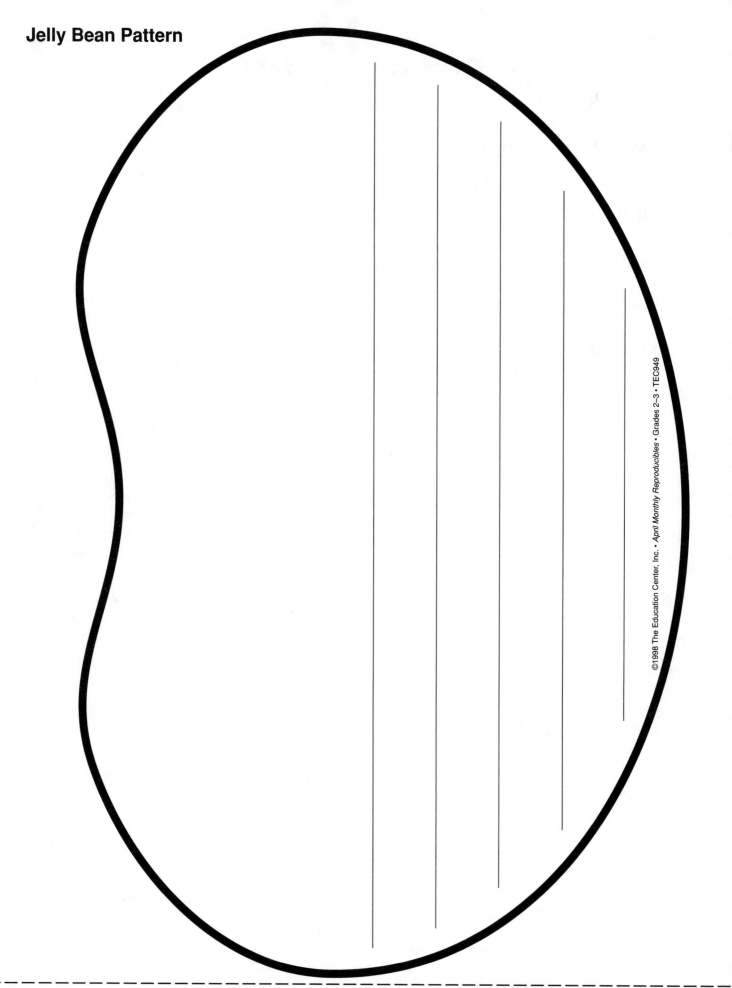

©1998 The Education Center, Inc. • *April Monthly Reproducibles* • Grades 2–3 • TEC949

**Note To The Teacher:** Use with "Jovial Jelly Beans" on page 25.

Name _____

# Colorful Fractions

## Fractional Parts Of Sets

1.  How many jelly beans are in your set?_____
    (This number will be your denominator.)

2.  What fractional part of your set is **red?**_____

3.  What fractional part of your set is **orange?**_____

4.  What fractional part of your set is **yellow?**_____

5.  What fractional part of your set is **green?**_____

6.  What fractional part of your set is **purple?**_____

7.  What fractional part of your set is **pink?**_____

8.  What fractional part of your set is **white?**_____

9.  What fractional part of your set is **black?**_____

## Adding Fractions

10. What fractional part of the set are the red and orange jelly beans? Add the fractions to find out._____

11. What fractional part of the set are the white and black jelly beans? Add the fractions to find out._____

12. What fractional part of the set are the pink and purple jelly beans? Add the fractions to find out._____

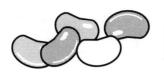

**Bonus Box:**
If you put all your jelly beans into a bag and picked one without looking, which color would you **probably** pick? Write about your answer on the back of this paper.

**Note To The Teacher:** Use with "Fun With Fractions" on page 25.

# Baskets Of Beans

Read the directions under each basket.
Then color the jelly beans.

**1**

Color **2/8** of the beans **blue**.
Color 3/8 of the beans **red**.
Color 1/8 of the beans **green**.
Color 2/8 of the beans **yellow**.

**2**

Color **2/5** of the beans **black**.
Color **3/5** of the beans **orange**.

**3**

Color **3/4** of the beans **orange**.
Color **1/4** of the beans **green**.

**4**

Color **2/6** of the beans **red**.
Color **3/6** of the beans **green**.
Color **1/6** of the beans **pink**.

**Bonus Box:** Look at Basket 1. What fraction of the beans is **not** yellow? Write your answer on the back of this paper.

# Bunnies, Bunnies, Bunnies!

"Every-bunny" loves bunnies! And your youngsters will, too!
Get a jump on springtime with these beloved bunny activities!

## Bouncing Bunnies

Get youngsters hopping down the bunny trail when they practice prefix skills. Each student will need one copy of the gameboard, game markers, spinner, and wheel patterns on pages 31 and 32. Have each child color her gameboard and glue it to a 9" x 12" sheet of construction paper. Next direct her to tape a zippered plastic bag to the back of her project. Have each student color and cut out the two game-marker patterns, then fold and glue them as shown to make upright game markers. Have her color and cut out the spinner and wheel patterns; then direct her to punch a hole at the dot on the spinner and attach the spinner to the wheel with a brad. To play the game, divide students into pairs. Instruct students to read the directions on their gameboards and to check each answer with a provided dictionary. Invite youngsters to store their game pieces in the zippered bags and take the games home to play with family members.

For additional prefix skills practice, provide each youngster with a white construction-paper copy of the carrot pattern on page 32. Have her write her name on the line. Then instruct her to select two words she made in the game and write a sentence for each one on her carrot pattern. Next direct her to lightly color and then cut out her pattern. Provide time for students to share their sentences with their classmates.

Alicia
name

My sister will misplace her toothbrush today. My dad reset the VCR.

## Funny Bunnies

These funny bunnies are just what you need for some creative-writing practice! Challenge students to brainstorm words or phrases that describe bunnies; then list their responses on the chalkboard. Instruct each child to write a funny bunny story on a sheet of writing paper, incorporating some of the words from the list. Next provide each youngster with a copy of the bunny parts on page 30. Direct him to color the bunny parts and cut them out. Have him glue the bunny parts to his writing paper as shown. Invite each child to share his funny bunny story with classmates; then display the stories around the room for all to enjoy!

One day I saw two bunnies. They were hopping in the grass. I fed them some carrots and rubbed their fluffy white fur.

**Bunny Parts**

**Note To The Teacher:** Use with "Funny Bunnies" on page 29.

# Bouncing Bunnies

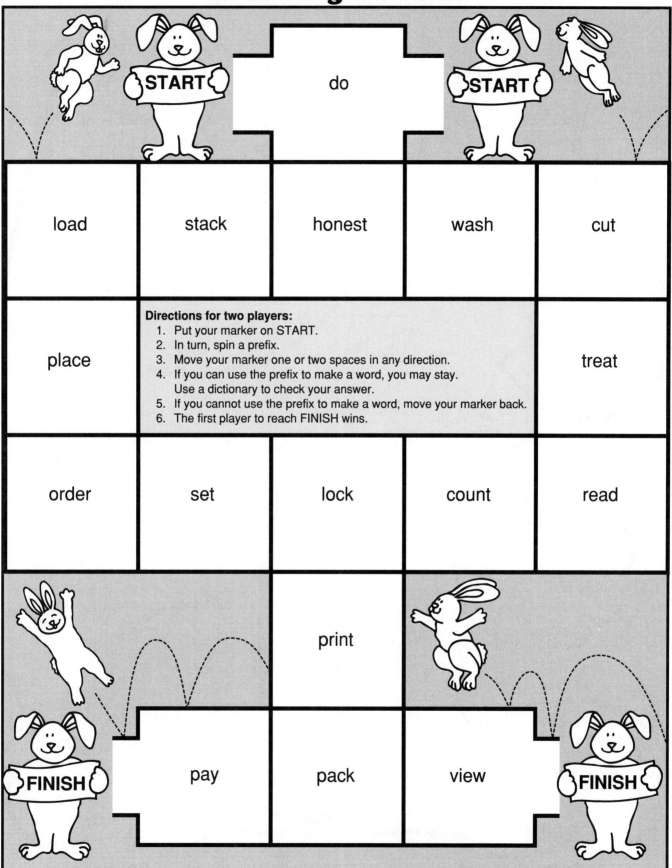

START

do

START

load

stack

honest

wash

cut

place

**Directions for two players:**
1. Put your marker on START.
2. In turn, spin a prefix.
3. Move your marker one or two spaces in any direction.
4. If you can use the prefix to make a word, you may stay.
   Use a dictionary to check your answer.
5. If you cannot use the prefix to make a word, move your marker back.
6. The first player to reach FINISH wins.

treat

order

set

lock

count

read

print

FINISH

pay

pack

view

FINISH

**Note To The Teacher:** Use with "Bouncing Bunnies" on page 29.

# Game Markers, Spinner, And Wheel

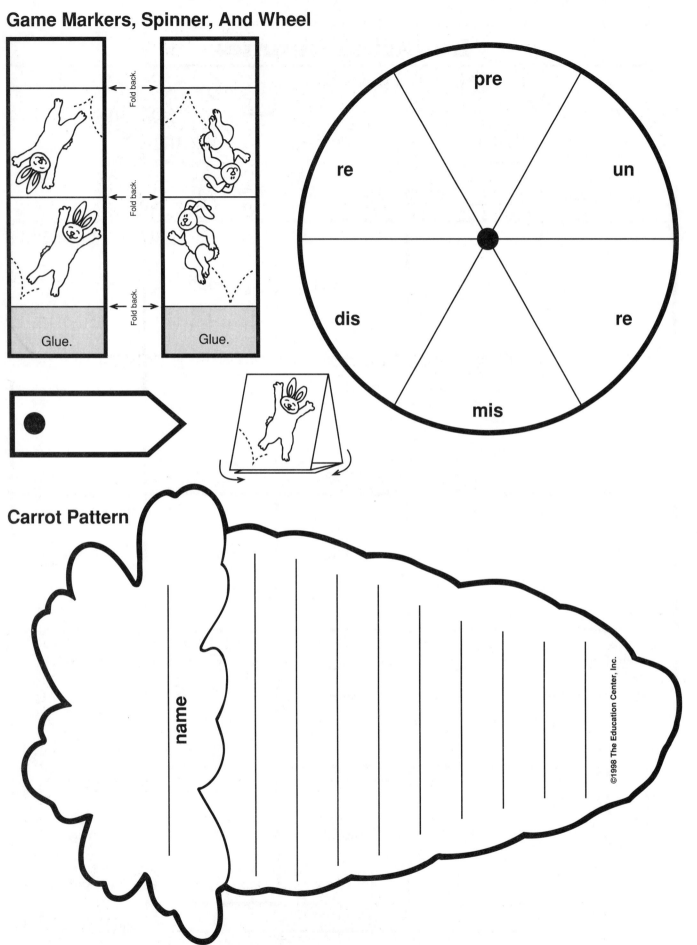

Fold back.
Fold back.
Fold back.

Glue.

Glue.

pre

re

un

dis

re

mis

## Carrot Pattern

name

**Note To The Teacher:** Use with "Bouncing Bunnies" on page 29.

# "EGG-STRA" SPECIAL!

Spring is the season of many new life cycles, from hatching chicks to baby ducklings. Check out this selection of "eggs-tra"-special ways to give your students something to chirp about!

## Look What Hatched!

Expand your students' knowledge about animals that hatch from eggs with this student-made bulletin-board display. Prior to the activity, place a picture (or small toy) of an animal that hatches from an egg inside a plastic egg. To begin, share with students a book about animals that hatch from eggs. Next show the prepared egg to your students, and initiate a discussion of the types of creatures that hatch from eggs (such as insects, reptiles, amphibians, birds, and fish). Give your students a clue about the animal inside the plastic egg, and solicit several guesses before revealing the contents. Next distribute two large, egg-shaped cutouts to each student. Instruct each child to write a clue about an animal that hatches from an egg on the first cutout and draw a picture of it on the second cutout. Have each student staple his clue atop his completed drawing; then mount the egg projects on a bulletin board titled "Look What Hatched!" Encourage your students to visit the display to read each clue and guess the animal that is waiting behind its shell.

I have a shell on my back. What am I?

## What's Inside?

Sharpen students' investigation skills with this "egg-citing" game. In advance collect and number an assortment of plastic eggs. Fill pairs of eggs with different types of material, such as dried beans, wood shavings, paper clips, pennies, or marbles. Seal the two halves of each egg together with tape. Next pair students; then randomly give each pair a different egg. Challenge each pair to find its matching egg. To do this, students gently shake the eggs as they walk around the room. When students believe they have found their match, invite each pair to "crack" the eggs open over a bowl or placemat to reveal the contents. Reward each youngster with a small chocolate egg or other treat for his participation.

From Egg To Chick

## From Egg To Chick

Help your students make "egg-cellent" mobiles to illustrate the life cycle of a baby chick. Duplicate a class set of "Chick Mobile" on page 36 on white construction paper. Distribute a copy of the activity page, another sheet of white construction paper, and an egg-shaped template to each student. To create a mobile, the student colors the pictures and cuts out the nine pieces. (If desired, have each child reinforce the hen-and-chick pattern by gluing it onto tagboard and cutting it out a second time.) Using her template, the student traces and cuts out four egg shapes from white construction paper. Next she matches each of the written stages of the egg-to-chick development with the corresponding picture. She then glues the matching pair to an egg cutout so that the picture is on the front of the egg and the text is on the back. Help her hole-punch the eggs; then have her use yarn to connect the pieces in the correct sequence. Suspend the completed projects from your classroom ceiling for a cheerful chick display.

**Chick Mobile**

From Egg To Chick

©1998 The Education Center, Inc. • *April Monthly Reproducibles* • Grades 2-3 • TEC949

| A hen lays an egg. She sits on the egg to keep it warm. | A baby chick grows inside the shell for about 21 days. | The chick pecks its way out of the shell with its beak. | The chick's wet body will soon dry. It will have short, fluffy feathers. |
|---|---|---|---|
| 1 | 2 | 3 | 4 |

**Note To The Teacher:** Use with "From Egg To Chick" on page 35.

# A Delightful Dozen

Read each sentence.
Decide if it tells a fact or an opinion.
Use the code to color the matching eggs.

Which is **fact** and which is **opinion**?

1. Some baby animals hatch from eggs.
2. Butterflies lay their eggs on plants.
3. Butterflies are prettier than caterpillars.
4. A spider can lay up to 3,000 eggs in one egg sac.
5. Ducks also lay eggs.
6. Baby ducks are so cute!
7. Some sharks lay eggs in leathery shells.
8. We have many uses for chicken eggs.
9. It's fun to color eggs for Easter.
10. Scrambled eggs are good for breakfast.
11. Cakes and cookies are made with eggs.
12. Hard-boiled eggs are a treat.

**Color Code:**
Fact—yellow
Opinion—brown

**Bonus Box:** On the back of this paper, list a dozen different ways to eat eggs.

# Happy Hatchers

Read the facts about some egg-laying animals.
Circle their names in the puzzle below.
Put a check by each fact as you find the animal's name.
Then color each animal's picture.

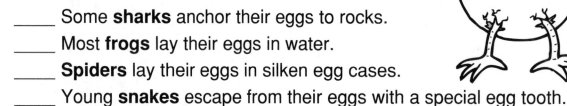

_____ Some **sharks** anchor their eggs to rocks.

_____ Most **frogs** lay their eggs in water.

_____ **Spiders** lay their eggs in silken egg cases.

_____ Young **snakes** escape from their eggs with a special egg tooth.

_____ **Ostrich** eggs are larger than those of any other bird.

_____ Some **turtles** lay 200 to 300 eggs at a time.

_____ **Alligators** cover their eggs with mud and wet leaves.

_____ Certain **fish** lay millions of eggs in their lifetimes.

_____ **Butterflies** and **moths** lay small, tough-shelled eggs.

| o | a | p | f | r | o | g | s | b | b | c |
| s | d | r | i | e | s | g | f | t | u | g |
| t | h | u | s | a | i | v | b | j | t | w |
| r | k | s | h | a | r | k | s | l | t | m |
| i | n | x | c | o | q | d | n | p | e | q |
| c | r | e | m | s | i | t | a | f | r | u |
| h | v | l | w | h | y | o | k | x | f | y |
| z | m | o | t | h | s | a | e | b | l | c |
| d | s | p | i | d | e | r | s | e | i | f |
| g | n | g | h | j | o | z | i | j | e | k |
| l | k | m | t | u | r | t | l | e | s | n |
| p | a | l | l | i | g | a | t | o | r | s |

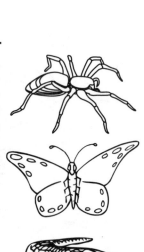

**Bonus Box:** On the back of this paper, draw a picture of another animal that lays eggs.

# A Dozen Describing Words

Read the words on each egg.
Draw a crack through the *adjective* on each egg.

1. egg
   hard

Remember:
an adjective is
a **describing**
word.

2. beak
   sharp

3. yolk
   yellow

4. red
   hen

5. chick
   fluffy

6. claws
   strong

7. brown
   nest

8. rooster
   large

9. eyes
   tiny

10. smooth
    shell

11. feathers
    soft

12. peep
    noisy

**Bonus Box:** Choose three of the adjectives from above. Write a sentence with each one on the back of this paper.

# Roll Call!

Help Mother Hen check on her chicks.
Write the names in ABC order to see who's missing.

Blackie
Pete
Flappy
Chuck
Chirper
Pesky
Blinky
Fluffy
Cheeps
Pecky
Flip
Blue

1. _____

2. _____

3. _____

4. _____

5. _____

6. _____

7. _____

8. _____

9. _____

10. _____

11. _____

12. _____

Which chick is missing? _____

**Bonus Box:** On the back of this paper, draw a picture to show where the missing chick was hiding.

©1998 The Education Center, Inc. • *April Monthly Reproducibles* • Grades 2–3 • TEC949 • Key p. 63

# National Library Week

Sponsored by the American Library Association, National Library Week honors librarians, libraries, and the pleasures of reading. Encourage your little bookworms to read when they celebrate National Library Week in April.

## Book Bonanza!

This book bonanza is just what you need to motivate young readers! Ask each youngster to borrow a book from the library for a book report project. Then provide each student with a white construction-paper copy of the book report form on page 42 and one extra sheet of white construction paper. After reading his book, each child should complete the page, color it as desired, and then cut the form out along the bold line. Next have him trace around his form onto his other sheet of construction paper and cut out the form. Instruct each student to illustrate his favorite part on the cutout. Have him complete the project by putting his report form atop his picture and stapling the two together along the left side. Invite students to share their book reports with their classmates; then collect the projects and staple them to a bulletin board titled "Book Bonanza!"

## Bona Fide Bookworms

Turn your youngsters into bona fide bookworms with this reading incentive. In advance, cut one green construction-paper worm for each student. Write each child's name on a worm; then mount the worms on a wall or bulletin board titled "Bona Fide Bookworms." To begin, ask students if they can tell you what the term *bookworm* means; then share with them that a bookworm is someone who is devoted to reading. Tell students that they, too, can become bookworms by reading a lot of books. Set a reading goal for your class (or for individual students); then give each student one copy of the reading log on page 43. Direct each youngster to read at home daily and record it on her log. Collect the logs at the end of the week. Each time she meets her reading goal, place a small star or sticker on her worm. When each youngster has earned a predetermined number of stars, reward her with a copy of the reading award on page 44.

## Bookworm's Booklist

Any bookworm is sure to love these stories with a library theme!

- *Cam Jansen & The Mystery Of The Chocolate Fudge Sale* by David A. Adler (Viking Children's Books, 1993)
- *How To Live Forever* by Colin Thompson (Alfred A. Knopf, Inc.; 1996)
- *Tomás And The Library Lady* by Pat Mora (Alfred A. Knopf, Inc.; 1997)

# Book Report

The name of my book is _____.

It was written by _____.

The book is about _____

_____

_____

_____

My favorite part is _____

_____

_____

I _____ recommend this book because _____
  (would/would not)

_____

_____

_____

Name _____

# I Read At Home

| Day | Today I read | I read to |
|-----|--------------|-----------|
| Monday | | |
| Tuesday | | |
| Wednesday | | |
| Thursday | | |
| Friday | | |
| Saturday | | |
| Sunday | | |

Name _____

# I Read At Home

| Day | Today I read | I read to |
|-----|--------------|-----------|
| Monday | | |
| Tuesday | | |
| Wednesday | | |
| Thursday | | |
| Friday | | |
| Saturday | | |
| Sunday | | |

**Note To The Teacher:** Use with "Bona Fide Bookworms" on page 41.

# Way To Go

_____ !

You are a bona fide
bookworm!

_____     _____
teacher signature                                    date

©1998 The Education Center, Inc. • _April Monthly Reproducibles_ • Grades 2–3 • TEC949

# Way To Go

_____ !

You are a bona fide
bookworm!

_____     _____
teacher signature                                    date

©1998 The Education Center, Inc. • _April Monthly Reproducibles_ • Grades 2–3 • TEC949

# Busy Bookworms

Help the bookworm put the books on the shelves.
Cut out the books below.
Glue them in ABC order on the shelves.

| 1. | 2. | 3. | 4. | 5. | 6. |
|---|---|---|---|---|---|
| | | | | | |

| 7. | 8. | 9. | 10. | 11. | 12. |
|---|---|---|---|---|---|
| | | | | | |

**Bonus Box:** Choose a book from the list. On the back of this page, draw a picture of what a page in the book might look like; then write two sentences to go with your picture.

Name _____

# Bookworm Balance

Rewrite each set of numbers.
Order the numbers from the least to the greatest.

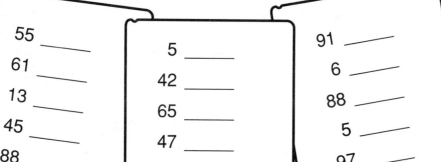

55 _____
61 _____
13 _____
45 _____
88 _____

5 _____
42 _____
65 _____
47 _____
33 _____

91 _____
6 _____
88 _____
5 _____
97 _____

41 _____
64 _____
52 _____
70 _____
35 _____

15 _____
9 _____
31 _____
55 _____
49 _____

21 _____
4 _____
25 _____
67 _____
61 _____

37 _____
41 _____
69 _____
28 _____
23 _____

81 _____
86 _____
80 _____
85 _____
82 _____

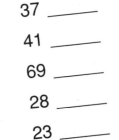

19 _____
24 _____
16 _____
9 _____
34 _____

**Bonus Box:** Circle the odd numbers in blue. Draw a red box around the even numbers.

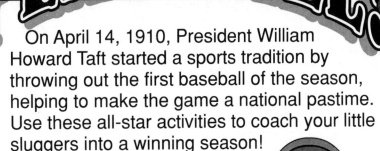

# PLAY BALL!

On April 14, 1910, President William Howard Taft started a sports tradition by throwing out the first baseball of the season, helping to make the game a national pastime. Use these all-star activities to coach your little sluggers into a winning season!

## Baseball Diamantes

Help your students take a swing at poetry with this innovative writing activity! Begin by writing "BASEBALL" on the chalkboard. Ask students to name words that describe baseball; then list their responses on the chalkboard. Next distribute one copy of the writing pattern (page 48) to each student. Direct each youngster to refer to the list as he writes a diamante poem by following the format at right. Next have each child cut out his pattern, glue it onto a slightly larger piece of construction paper, and trim the paper to create an eye-catching border. Provide time for students to share their poems with their classmates; then mount the poems on a bulletin board titled "Let's Hear It For Baseball!"

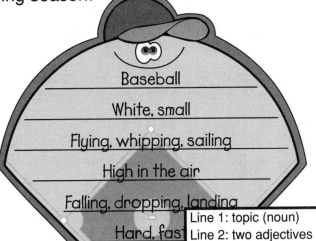

Baseball
White, small
Flying, whipping, sailing
High in the air
Falling, dropping, landing
Hard, fast
Baseball

Line 1: topic (noun)
Line 2: two adjectives
Line 3: three action words
Line 4: a four-word phrase
Line 5: three action words
Line 6: two adjectives
Line 7: rename the topic

## What A Hit!

Your youngsters will think this learning center is a real hit! Duplicate one construction-paper copy of the bear pattern and ten construction-paper copies of the baseball hat pattern on page 49. Color the bear as desired; then cut it out and glue it to the front of a manila envelope titled "What A Hit!" Next program each hat with a different word problem. Store the hats and an answer key in the envelope. To use the center, a student removes the hats from the envelope, solves the problems on a sheet of paper, and then checks his answers with the key. To provide youngsters will additional skills practice, simply duplicate additional copies of the hat, and then program them with addition or subtraction problems, or with vocabulary words to be placed in ABC order.

## All-Star Wrap-Up!

Score a home run with your students when you wrap up your unit with this all-star idea! Invite each child to wear a baseball cap of her favorite team to school. Next sing the well-known song "Take Me Out To The Ball Game!" with your students; then share a story with a baseball theme. Serve a snack of baseball foods, such as peanuts, popcorn, and soda; then have youngsters illustrate pennants of their favorite books on triangle cutouts to display around the room.

The Baseball Star
by
Fred G. Arrigg, Jr.

# Writing Pattern

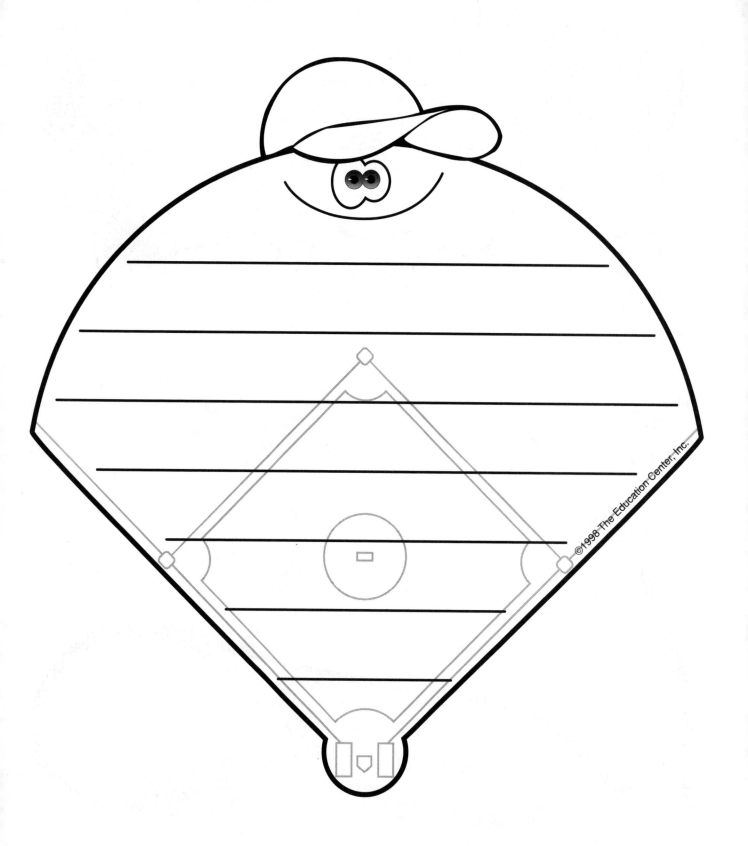

**Note To The Teacher:** Use with "Baseball Diamantes" on page 47.

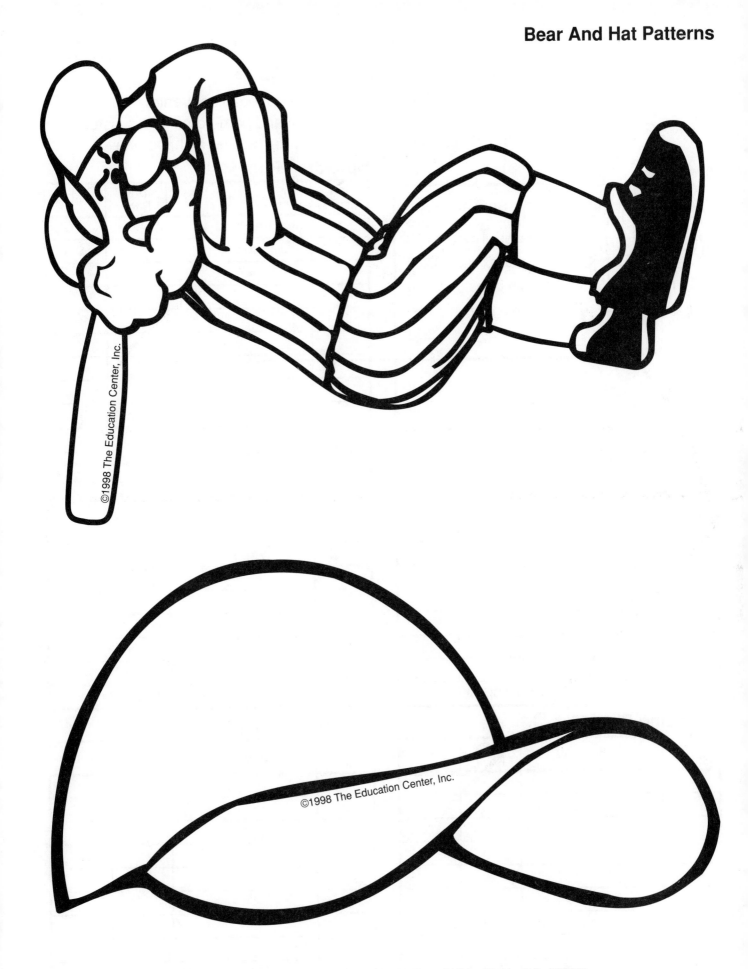

©1998 The Education Center, Inc.

©1998 The Education Center, Inc.

**Note To The Teacher:** Use with "What A Hit!" on page 47.

# Baseball Souvenirs

Buddy Bear has $10.00 to spend on baseball souvenirs.
He is buying a baseball bat for himself and pom-poms for his sister.
Show five different ways that Buddy can spend all his money.

### Souvenirs

| | |
|---|---|
| baseball bat | $4.00 |
| baseball cap | $3.00 |
| pom-poms | $2.00 |
| trading cards | $1.00 |
| pennant | $.75 |
| baseball | $.50 |
| program | $.50 |
| poster | $.25 |

## Spending Plan #1

| How Many? | Item | Unit Price | Total |
|---|---|---|---|
| 1 | baseball bat | 4.00 | 4.00 |
| 1 | pom-poms | 2.00 | 2.00 |
| | | | |
| | | | |
| | | | |
| | | | |
| | | | |
| | | | |
| | | **Total Spent** | |

## Spending Plan #2

| How Many? | Item | Unit Price | Total |
|---|---|---|---|
| | | | |
| | | | |
| | | | |
| | | | |
| | | | |
| | | | |
| | | | |
| | | | |
| | | **Total Spent** | |

## Spending Plan #3

| How Many? | Item | Unit Price | Total |
|---|---|---|---|
| | | | |
| | | | |
| | | | |
| | | | |
| | | | |
| | | | |
| | | | |
| | | | |
| | | **Total Spent** | |

## Spending Plan #4

| How Many? | Item | Unit Price | Total |
|---|---|---|---|
| | | | |
| | | | |
| | | | |
| | | | |
| | | | |
| | | | |
| | | | |
| | | **Total Spent** | |

## Spending Plan #5

| How Many? | Item | Unit Price | Total |
|---|---|---|---|
| | | | |
| | | | |
| | | | |
| | | | |
| | | | |
| | | | |
| | | | |
| | | **Total Spent** | |

# Batter Up!

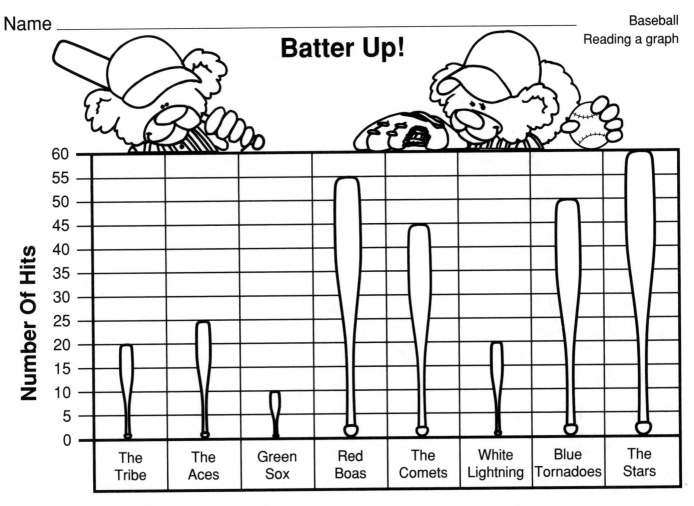

Number Of Hits

| | The Tribe | The Aces | Green Sox | Red Boas | The Comets | White Lightning | Blue Tornadoes | The Stars |

Answer the questions.
Use the graph.

1. Which team made 45 hits? _____

2. Which two teams made more hits than the Blue Tornadoes? _____

3. How many hits did The Aces make? _____

4. Which two teams made the same number of hits? _____

5. Which two teams made more hits than The Comets and fewer hits than The Stars? _____

6. How many more hits did The Stars make than White Lightning? _____

7. Which team had the least number of hits? _____

8. How many more hits did the Red Boas make than The Tribe? _____

**Bonus Box:** How many hits did The Stars, The Comets, and the Blue Tornadoes make altogether? Solve the problem on the back of this paper.

Name _____

Baseball
Multiplication

# Baseball Bonanza!

Solve each fact.
Cut out the baseballs below.
Put a drop of glue on each ●.
Then glue each ball to its matching mitt.

1.
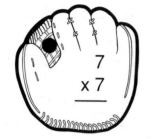
$\begin{array}{r} 7 \\ \times\, 7 \\ \hline \end{array}$

2.
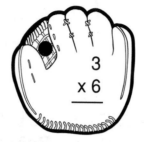
$\begin{array}{r} 3 \\ \times\, 6 \\ \hline \end{array}$

3.
$\begin{array}{r} 7 \\ \times\, 8 \\ \hline \end{array}$

4.
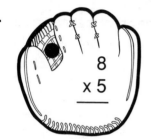
$\begin{array}{r} 8 \\ \times\, 5 \\ \hline \end{array}$

5.
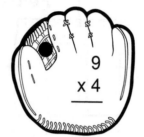
$\begin{array}{r} 9 \\ \times\, 4 \\ \hline \end{array}$

6.
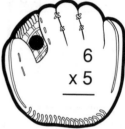
$\begin{array}{r} 6 \\ \times\, 5 \\ \hline \end{array}$

7.
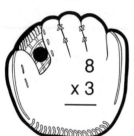
$\begin{array}{r} 8 \\ \times\, 3 \\ \hline \end{array}$

8.
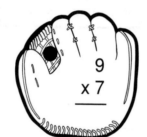
$\begin{array}{r} 9 \\ \times\, 7 \\ \hline \end{array}$

9.
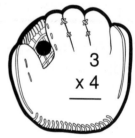
$\begin{array}{r} 3 \\ \times\, 4 \\ \hline \end{array}$

10.
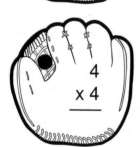
$\begin{array}{r} 4 \\ \times\, 4 \\ \hline \end{array}$

11.
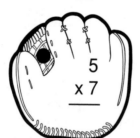
$\begin{array}{r} 5 \\ \times\, 7 \\ \hline \end{array}$

12.
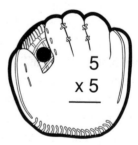
$\begin{array}{r} 5 \\ \times\, 5 \\ \hline \end{array}$

©1998 The Education Center, Inc. • *April Monthly Reproducibles* • Grades 2–3 • TEC949 • Key p. 64

 35    63    40    49    36   12

 24    18    30    16   25   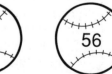 56

# Birds Of A Feather

Birds come in all shapes, sizes, and colors—ranging from the two-inch bee hummingbird to the eight-foot ostrich. And birds can be found as far away as Antarctica or as close as students' own backyards. Pique your little ornithologists' interest in birds with this flock of activities.

## Peacock Pride

Peacocks are known for showing off their best feature—their tail feathers. Invite your students to show off their best features with this peacock project. Duplicate one white construction-paper copy of the peacock patterns (page 54) for each student. Have him write one word that describes himself at the wide end of each of his feathers. Next have him write his name on the line, lightly color his peacock and feather patterns as desired, and then cut them out. Direct him to attach the feathers to the body of the peacock by pushing a large brad though the dot on the body, and then through the dot on each feather. Invite students to share their peacocks with their classmates. Then collect the projects and mount them on a bulletin board titled "Peacock Pride."

## Warble Away!

Introduce your warblers to bird calls with this "trilling" idea! To begin, tell students that birds use their voices to communicate with one another through calls and songs. Calls are used for warnings or to keep in contact with a group of birds. Songs are used mainly to attract a mate or to advertise the ownership of territory. Next share the bird calls shown. Invite students to practice saying the calls aloud. Then have youngsters play this bird-calling game. Randomly (and secretly) assign each student a different bird call. (Each call may be assigned to several students.) Instruct each child to softly speak his bird call as he walks around the room. Have students form flocks when they hear students with the same call. When all youngsters have joined a flock, reassign the bird calls and play the game again.

Chickadee—chicka-dee, dee, dee
Dove—coo, coo
Mallard—quack, quack
Goose—honk, honk
Owl—hoot, hoot
Catbird—meow, meow
Crow—caw, caw
Whippoorwill—whip-poor-will

## Bird Acrostics

Wrap up your study of birds with these bird acrostics. To begin, have students brainstorm the names of different birds. List their responses on the chalkboard. Next have each child select a different bird and use capital letters to write its name down the left side of a sheet of drawing paper. Instruct the student to write a descriptive word or phrase that begins with each letter in the name. Allow time for students to decorate their work. If desired collect the papers and staple them between two construction-paper covers. Add a title such as "Birds, Birds, Birds!," a class byline, and desired decorations to the front cover.

Clever bird
Really black feathers
Opens its beak
Wants to eat corn
and bugs

# Peacock Patterns

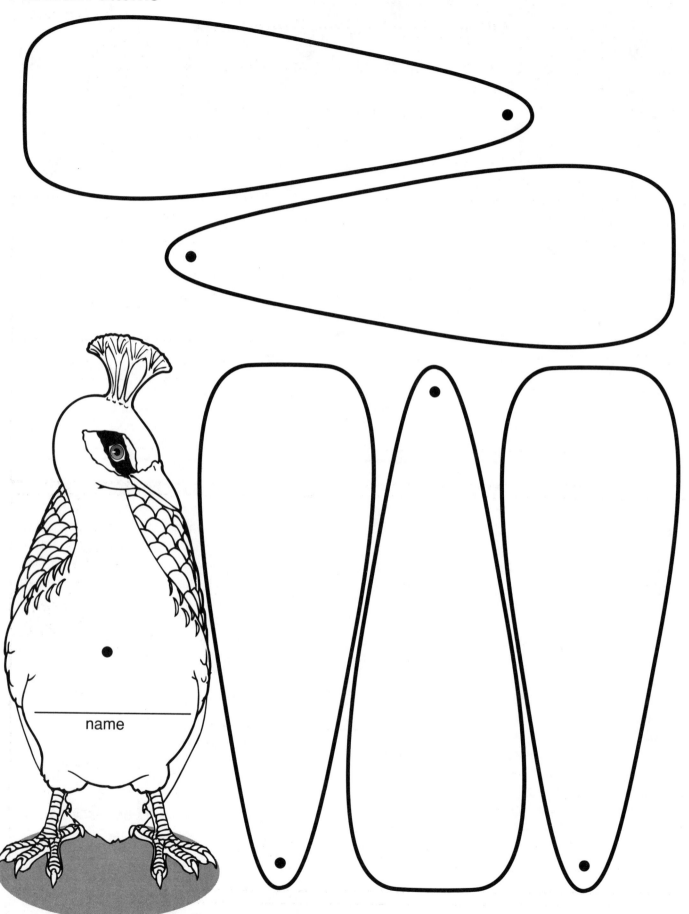

name

**Note To The Teacher:** Use with "Peacock Pride" on page 53.

# Migrating Word Problems

Gordon Goose is traveling south for the
    winter.
Find how many miles Gordon will travel.
Solve each problem using the map below.
Show your work.

How many miles is it from:

| | | |
|---|---|---|
| 1. Mount Freeze to Rainytown?<br><br><br>+_____ | 2. Coldville to Misty Valley?<br><br><br>+_____ | 3. Rainytown to Middleburg?<br><br><br>+_____ |
| 4. Middleburg to Sunshine Land?<br><br><br>+_____ | 5. Pleasant City to Hot Town?<br><br><br>+_____ | 6. Sunshine Land to Summer Beach?<br><br><br>+_____ |

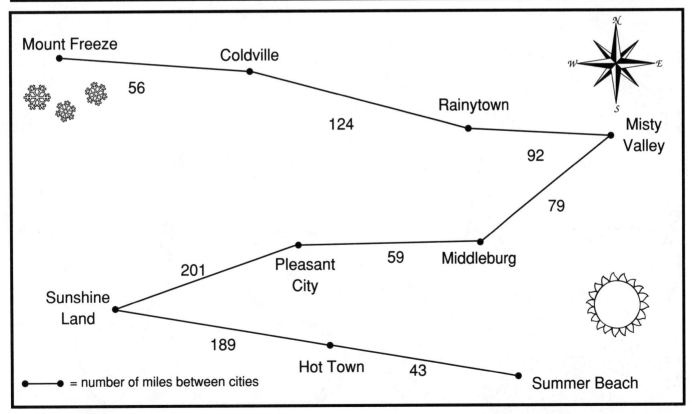

●——● = number of miles between cities

**Bonus Box:** On the back of this page, write three new problems; then give them to a friend to solve.

# Carly Cuckoo's Contractions

Cut out the eggs below.
Put a drop of glue on each ● .
Glue each egg to its matching word pair.

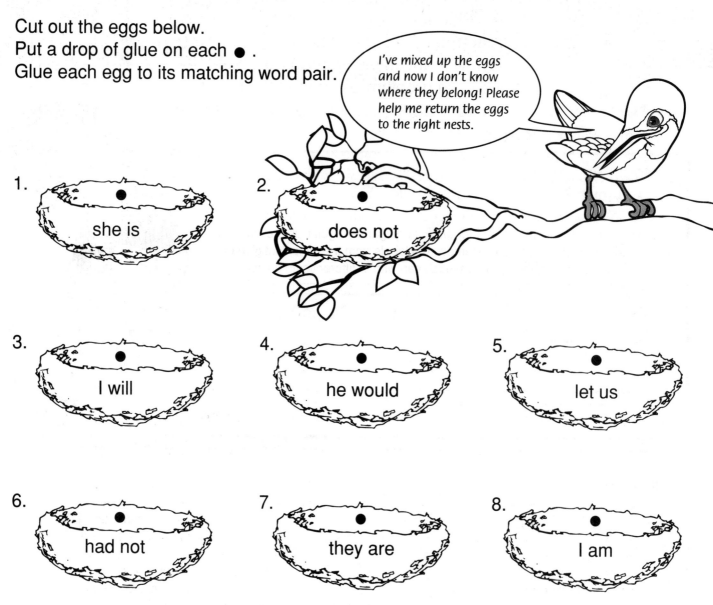

I've mixed up the eggs and now I don't know where they belong! Please help me return the eggs to the right nests.

1. she is

2. does not

3. I will

4. he would

5. let us

6. had not

7. they are

8. I am

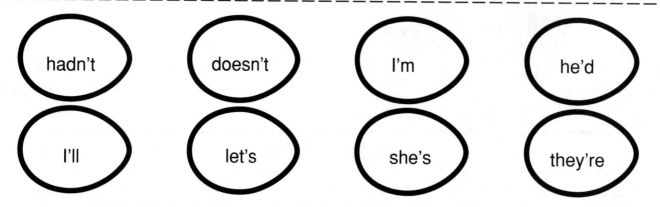

hadn't    doesn't    I'm    he'd

I'll    let's    she's    they're

**Bonus Box:** Choose five contractions from above. Write a sentence for each one on the back of this page.

# Mathematics Education Month

## April is Mathematics Education Month

Get ready for a round of math skills! These activities will keep your students up to par with addition, subtraction, and other basic operations.

### Golfing Adds Up!

Want to put some excitement into adding coin amounts? Then this activity will suit your students to a tee! To prepare for the activity, gather a golf club, several golf balls, and five empty soup cans. Remove the labels from the cans. Hot glue or tape the cans together; then program each can with a different coin amount. Lay the cans on the floor as shown. Have each child stand at a designated point and take three turns gently putting the balls into the open ends of the cans with the golf club. Keep score by having the student add the total amount for his round. Or have students play in teams and add up the team members' scores. For a variation on the game, assign each student or team a dollar amount and subtract the coin amount determined by each turn.

5¢  15¢  50¢  25¢  10¢

### Roll For The Hole

Take your students out on the greens for a little multiplication practice. Duplicate one copy of page 58 for each student. Next divide youngsters into groups of two or three; then provide each group with a die. To play, each student, in turn, rolls the die and multiplies the resulting number with the number on the flag. He records the score for the hole on his paper before handing the die to the next player. Play continues as students follow the path to each hole. When each player has completed the "course," he totals his individual score. Remind students that in golf the lowest score wins. For further practice, simply duplicate one copy of page 58; then change the numbers on the flags by whiting them out and programming them with new numbers. Fore!

### Going For Distance

Enhance your students' measurement skills with a little putting practice. In advance, obtain a putter, several golf balls, and a tape measure. Take your class to the playground or to a carpeted area. Have each student gently putt a ball from a designated starting point. Assist her in measuring the distance from the starting point to her golf ball. If desired, record each distance; then have each student use the information to create a graph of putting distances, arrange the measurements in order from least to greatest, find the average of several different putts, or practice important skills.

# Roll For The Hole

# Caddy Snack Shack

The caddies are hungry after a long day on the golf course.
It's time to head for the Caddy Snack Shack!
Find the total of each caddy's order.

### Menu

| | |
|---|---|
| Putter Pizza $3.78 | Tee-Time Taco $1.88 |
| Nine-Iron Nachos $1.44 | Sand-Trap Shake $2.47 |
| Hole-In-One Hot Dog $2.25 | Fairway Fries $1.62 |
| Double-Bogey Burger $3.39 | Caddy Cola $1.06 |

1. **Birdie Bubba:**
Putter Pizza
Caddy Cola

+ _____

2. **Eagle Ed:**
Nine-Iron Nachos
Sand-Trap Shake

+ _____

3. **Bogey Bob:**
Tee-Time Taco
Fairway Fries

+ _____

4. **Drivin' Diane:**
Double-Bogey Burger
Sand-Trap Shake

+ _____

5. **Flyin' Fran:**
Hole-In-One Hot Dog
Caddy Cola

+ _____

6. **Teein' Tom:**
Fairway Fries
Sand-Trap Shake

+ _____

7. **Hole-In-One Hank:**
Putter Pizza
Sand-Trap Shake

+ _____

8. **Putterin' Patty:**
Tee-Time Taco
Nine-Iron Nachos

+ _____

9. **Outta' There Otto:**
Hole-In-One Hot Dog
Sand-Trap Shake

+ _____

10. **Up-To-Par Paul:**
Double-Bogey Burger
Fairway Fries

+ _____

11. **Nine-Iron Ned:**
Tee-Time Taco
Caddy Cola

+ _____

12. **Sand-Trap Sue:**
Putter Pizza
Hole-In-One Hot Dog

+ _____

**Bonus Box:** What would you order from the Caddy Snack Shack? Write your order on the back of this page; then add to find the total.

Name _____

# On The Green

Solve each problem.
Show your work.
Color the golf ball with the matching answer.

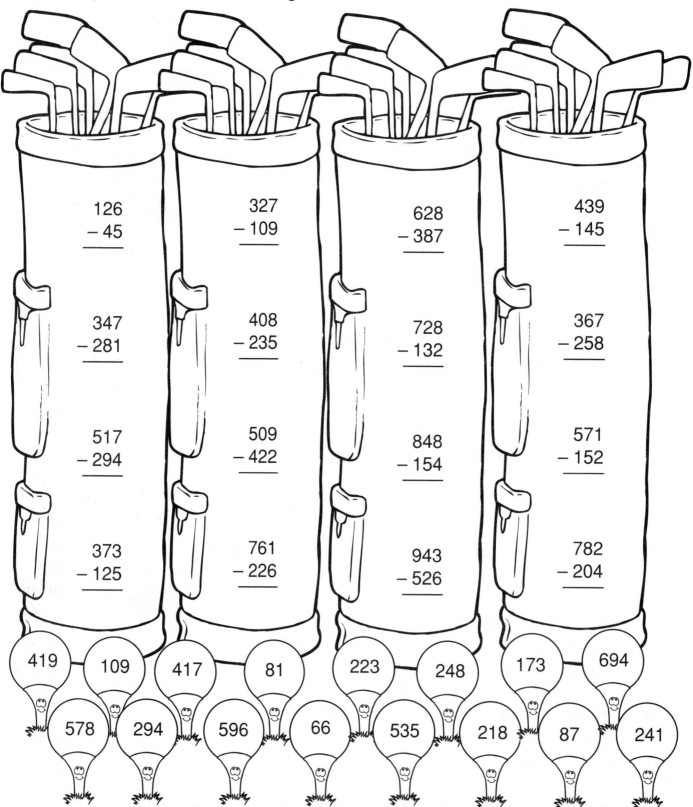

126
− 45
——

327
− 109
——

628
− 387
——

439
− 145
——

347
− 281
——

408
− 235
——

728
− 132
——

367
− 258
——

517
− 294
——

509
− 422
——

848
− 154
——

571
− 152
——

373
− 125
——

761
− 226
——

943
− 526
——

782
− 204
——

419    109    417    81    223    248    173    694

578    294    596    66    535    218    87    241

**Bonus Box:** On the back of this paper, list the numbers on the golf balls in order from *least* to *greatest*.

# Answer Keys

## Page 7
1. there's
2. he'll
3. won't
4. you've
5. she's
6. I'm
7. that's
8. haven't
9. who's
10. we've
11. they'd
12. can't

## Page 8
1. Lake Downpour
2. Mount Mallard
3. 12 inches
4. 22 inches
5. four inches
6. four inches
7. 48 inches

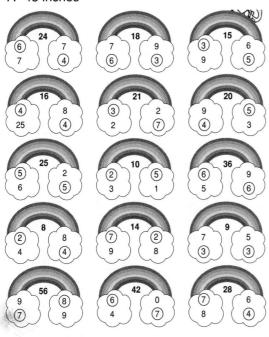

## Page 18

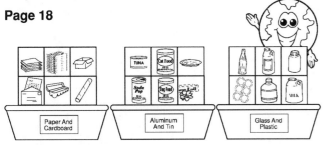

Paper And Cardboard

Aluminum And Tin

Glass And Plastic

## Page 23
**dictionary entry**
1. green line under: **tree**
2. yellow line under: (trē)
3. red circle around: *noun*
4. brown line under: A woody plant having a single main stem. It can reach heights of 20 to 25 feet and live for many years.
5. (Answers will vary.)

**guide words**
fig • grapefruit = fruit
redwood • rubber = root
apple • bark = banana
lime • nut = maple
beech • coconut = branch

## Page 33

| *less* | | *ness* | |
|---|---|---|---|
| lifeless | sleepless | sadness | sweetness |
| harmless | helpless | weakness | darkness |
| hopeless | careless | goodness | kindness |
| colorless | homeless | sickness | neatness |

## Page 34

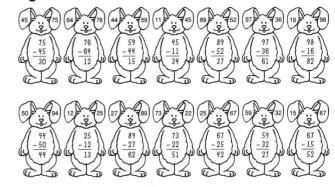

## Page 37
1. fact (yellow)
2. fact (yellow)
3. opinion (brown)
4. fact (yellow)
5. fact (yellow)
6. opinion (brown)
7. fact (yellow)
8. fact (yellow)
9. opinion (brown)
10. opinion (brown)
11. fact (yellow)
12. opinion (brown)

## Page 38

| o | a | p | f | r | o | g | s | b | b | c |
|---|---|---|---|---|---|---|---|---|---|---|
| s | d | r | i | e | s | g | f | t | u | g |
| t | h | u | s | a | i | v | b | j | t | w |
| r | k | s | h | a | r | k | s | l | t | m |
| i | n | x | c | o | q | d | n | p | e | q |
| c | r | e | m | s | i | t | a | f | r | u |
| h | v | l | w | h | y | o | k | x | f | y |
| z | m | o | t | h | s | a | e | b | l | c |
| d | s | p | i | d | e | r | s | e | i | f |
| g | n | g | h | j | o | z | i | j | e | k |
| l | k | m | t | u | r | t | l | e | s | n |
| p | a | l | l | i | g | a | t | o | r | s |

## Page 39
Cracks will be drawn through:
1. hard
2. sharp
3. yellow
4. red
5. fluffy
6. strong
7. brown
8. large
9. tiny
10. smooth
11. soft
12. noisy

## Page 40
1. Blackie
2. Blinky
3. Blue
4. Cheeps
5. Chirper
6. Chuck
7. Flappy
8. Flip
9. Fluffy
10. Pecky
11. Pesky
12. Pete
Which chick is missing? Pete

# Answer Keys

## Page 45
1. Betty's Backyard BBQ
2. Big Green Frogs
3. Lion And Turtle
4. Little Blue Dolphin
5. My Trip To China
6. Pebbles The Pig
7. Peekaboo Peacock
8. Sleepy Kitty
9. Soup Tales
10. Sunshine Days
11. Tell Me A Secret
12. Ten Until Bed

## Page 46

## Page 51
1. The Comets
2. Red Boas and The Stars
3. 25
4. The Tribe and White Lightning
5. Blue Tornadoes and Red Boas
6. 40
7. Green Sox
8. 35

**Bonus Box:** 155

## Page 52
| | | |
|---|---|---|
| 1. 49 | 5. 36 | 9. 12 |
| 2. 18 | 6. 30 | 10. 16 |
| 3. 56 | 7. 24 | 11. 35 |
| 4. 45 | 8. 63 | 12. 25 |

## Page 55
1. 56 + 124 = 180
2. 124 + 92 = 216
3. 92 + 79 = 171
4. 59 + 201 = 260
5. 201 + 189 = 390
6. 189 + 43 = 232

## Page 56
1. she's
2. doesn't
3. I'll
4. he'd
5. let's
6. hadn't
7. they're
8. I'm

## Page 59
| | |
|---|---|
| 1. $4.84 | 7. $6.25 |
| 2. $3.91 | 8. $3.32 |
| 3. $3.50 | 9. $4.72 |
| 4. $5.86 | 10. $5.01 |
| 5. $3.31 | 11. $2.94 |
| 6. $4.09 | 12. $6.03 |

## Page 60
| | | | |
|---|---|---|---|
| 81 | 218 | 241 | 294 |
| 66 | 173 | 596 | 109 |
| 223 | 87 | 694 | 419 |
| 248 | 535 | 417 | 578 |

**Bonus Box:** 66, 81, 87, 109, 173, 218, 223, 241, 248, 294, 417, 419, 535, 578, 596, 694

## Page 61
| | |
|---|---|
| 1. 2 golf balls | 5. 7 golf balls |
| 2. 3 golf balls | 6. 5 golf balls |
| 3. 4 golf balls | 7. 4 golf balls |
| 4. 6 golf balls | 8. 2 golf balls |

## Page 62
1. 30, 35, 40, 45
2. 90, 100, 110, 120
3. 24, 23, 22, 21
4. 28, 30, 32, 34
5. 70, 65, 60, 55
6. 500, 400, 300, 200
7. 84, 86, 88, 90
8. 18, 15, 12, 9
9. 24, 18, 12, 6
10. 42, 49, 56, 63